Maxine
Presents
The Crabbiest of
CRABBY ROAD

**Other MAXINE books from
Andrews McMeel Publishing**

SHOEBOX GREETINGS
(A tiny little division of Hallmark)

Hot Cider, Hot Cocoa and Hot Flashes: Maxine's Guide to the Holidays

Don't Worry, Be Crabby

Crabby Road

Other MAXINE books available through Hallmark

Aging Like a Fine Whiner

Maxine

Presents
The Crabbiest of
CRABBY ROAD

*Observations Guaranteed to Help You
Learn to  Your Attitude Problem, Too!*

Created by John M. Wagner

**Andrews McMeel
Publishing**

Kansas City

──────── **ATTENTION: SCHOOLS AND BUSINESSES** ────────

Andrews McMeel books are available at quantity discounts with bulk purchase for educational, business, or sales promotional use. For information, write to: Special Sales Department, Andrews McMeel Publishing, 4520 Main Street, Kansas City, Missouri 64111.

To all those women everywhere who were
the unknowing inspiration for "Maxine" . . .
and to the Shoebox writers who make her live . . .
thank you.

J. Wagner

—J. Wagner

My new low-fat diet is really working! The fat seems to hang lower every day.

Snowmen are like real men, only more attentive.

I believe in keeping
in shape.
I've chosen the shape
of an old lady.

You know those
restaurants where they
bring your dinner
and set it on fire?
How come no one
"oooohs" and "ahhhhs"
when I do that
at home?

I like to order pizza. Not only do you get good food, you can usually squeeze out enough grease to lube the car.

I once held up a supermarket... I wrote a check in the express lane.

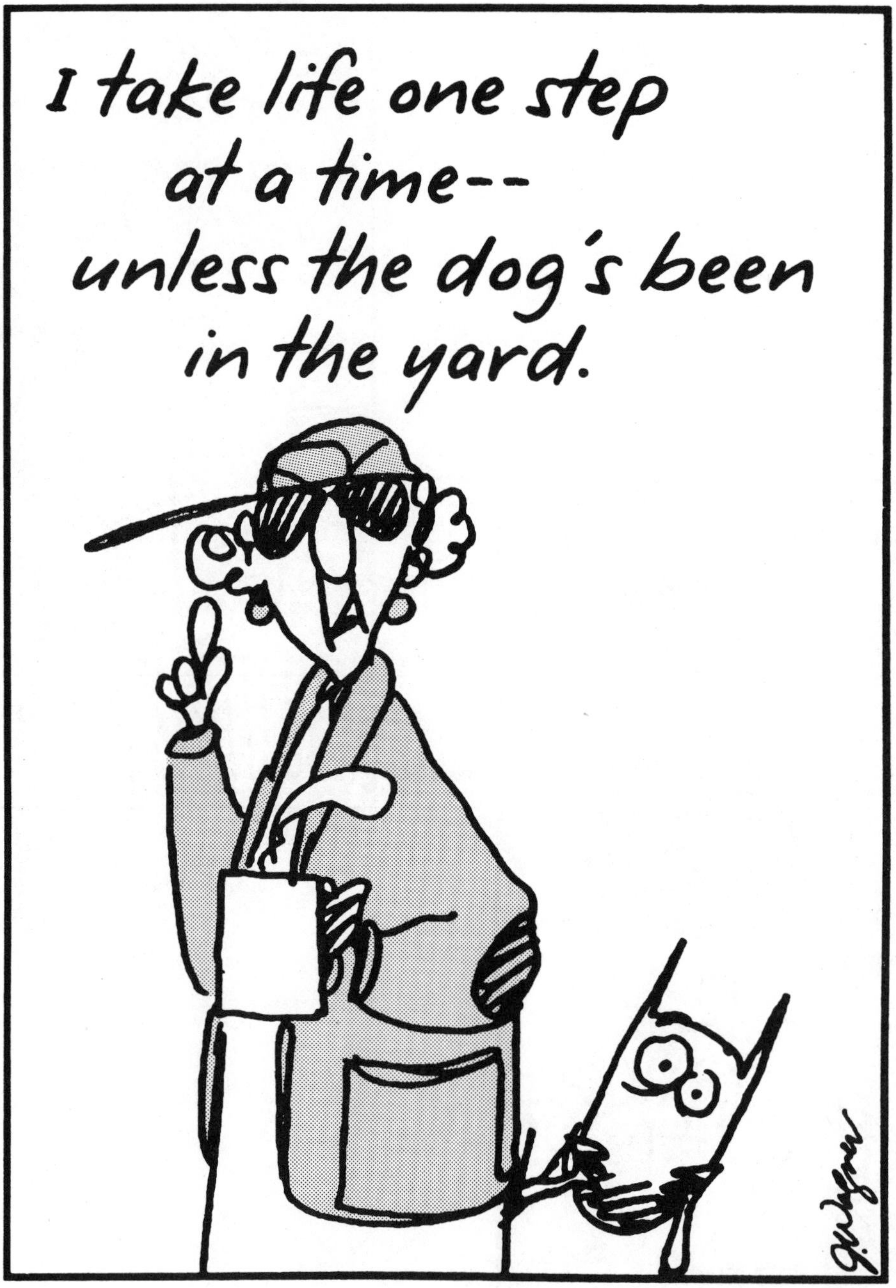
I take life one step at a time-- unless the dog's been in the yard.

It's time to fertilize the lawn, which means adding more fiber to the dog's diet.

I do my part to keep the planet green-- just look at my refrigerator.

I've been working with a personal trainer and it's great! I bring myself the paper and my slippers every morning.

Don't kill the messenger. Oh, and don't tip him, either.

Found a way to keep my cat from having accidents in the house. I don't let her drive.

See things my way, or be prepared to have your hat pulled over your face.

19

I like to go to drive-thru windows and order unhappy meals.

Why don't they have recycling centers where you could drop off your ex-husbands?

I figure, I don't cook my own food at restaurants, why should I pump my own gas at gas stations?

I love a good mystery. My favorite is "Why Are People Such Boneheads?"

Sure, I've got buns of steel... They're in the bread drawer.

I'll put a bird bath in my yard when the birds install a car wash in my garage.

My jaw really aches when I leave the dentist. Must be from keeping a straight face when I tell him I've been flossing.

If there's something I haven't used in five years, I give it to charity. But they probably don't need my in-laws' bad advice either.

I enjoy walking for exercise. A couple of times through my neighbor's flower garden usually does it.

Give peace a chance... Move to a new town and don't tell your relatives.

Never look a
gift horse
in the mouth,
and don't get too
close to the
other end,
either.

I recycle plastic.
Give me your
credit card and
I'll show
you how.

If I wanted to hear
the pitter-patter
of little feet,
I'd put shoes
on my cat.

The other day
I went to a psychic
and found out
what I was in
a previous life--
A total
pain.

Don't bite the hand that feeds you... not until you're full, anyway.

Life is what you make it. I make it unbearable for as many as possible.

Thought about having only fat-free weenies at my next cookout. But then I decided to go ahead and invite the relatives.

It's not what you do. It's what you get away with.

I believe in looking out for number one-- especially if the dog's not house-trained.

Old is just a state of behind.

One person's garbage is another person's treasure--
You don't mind if my dog digs through your treasure, do you?

I don't know much about baseball, but any game that involves throwing someone out can't be all bad!

I like to read in the bathroom. Especially if somebody's waitin' to get in there.

I say the lawn work's not over until you've thrown all the dandelions onto the neighbors' yards.

What's the big deal about centerfolds? My center has plenty of folds.

Brunch is for wimps who can't make up their minds.

The reason you can't fool all of the people all of the time, is because half of the people are women.

When they make a bagel with cream filling, frosting and sprinkles, I'll like them as well as doughnuts.

40

A winter cruise is a great opportunity to overeat while watching pale people turn beet-red.

Sometimes I like to ask the really big questions.
Why are we here?
What's the meaning of life?
What the heck are you lookin' at?

There's no fool like an old fool.
But the young ones are coming right along.

I finally found Mr. Right.
I call him up, he brings me pizza, and then he goes away.

Love makes the world
go round!
Course, eating bad
tuna makes it spin, too.

Men are like a box
of chocolates. You can
never tell which ones
are nuts.

I've got my own web site. It's in the corner near the ceiling. Darn Spiders.

Just bought a new pair of cross-trainers. So far, I've got the "cross" part down.

Life is like
the lottery:
Both are games of
chance, and both
involve a lot of
scratching.

You _can_ teach an
old dog a new trick
if "smell bad!" is
considered
a trick.

Tic-tac-toe is the perfect game for people who think checkers is too complicated.

There's no such thing as a "free offer." That's like saying "good banjo player."

Remember, "one size fits all" depends on your definition of "fits."

When the thigh cream bottle says "Not to be taken internally," you've got to wonder about some people.

I'd try to get my own
TV show, but I figure
I have to become a
mediocre comic first.

When I think of my
ex, I realize a fool
and his money never
got together in the
first place.

Vegetarianism is a fine concept, until it's just you and your cow on a desert island.

Those bulk candy stores are a great idea, if you like eating stuff a germy four-year-old was just putting his hands all over.

I always carry jumper cables in my car. It's fun to wave 'em at stranded motorists as I speed by.

Men are like small children...you bring a new one home, and the ones already there resent it.

I would plant my own vegetable garden, but you can't buy french fry seeds.

Why can't somebody invent a good self-cleaning floor?

Yeah, I've definitely
got spring fever.
Or a hot flash.
Hard to tell.

I don't really shop
from catalogs, but
it's so much fun to
make the mailman
deliver 'em.

Don't count your
chickens. And don't
blame my cat.
He has an
airtight
alibi.

When someone comes to the door selling something, I put shaving cream around my mouth and yell "Run! Run before the dog gets you, too!"

My eyes are waterin', my nose is runnin', I'm kinda itchy...either it's allergy season or one of the uncles has his shoes off.

Someday I'd like to take a train across America, but they never leave the keys in 'em.

Virtual mooning is nowhere near as rewarding.

With the new higher speed limits, I can shout insults at more drivers per hour than ever before.

I never use parking meters. The "time expired" sign gives me the creeps.

Kids can learn a lot about life from running a lemonade stand. Why just last week, a kid in my neighborhood learned what a lawsuit was when I choked on an ice cube.

I sleep in the nude. It's no big deal unless I nod off on the bus.

Happiness is where you find it. Maybe you should look someplace else.

Must be getting warmer...the mold in my shower is starting to bloom.

I'd enjoy lawn care, except for the part where you're supposed to care.

Ever see those kids on leashes in the mall? Why wouldn't that work for husbands?

If it weren't for baseball, we'd probably never see millionaires spit or scratch.

E-mail is for people who thought answering machines and memos weren't annoying enough.

If you're wearing a thong anywhere but on your feet, there's been a terrible mistake.

Bottled water is proof that anybody with a garden hose can become a millionaire.

Those ads for milk would look a lot better if the celebrities would wipe their mouths.

Often, when I get a parking ticket, it's followed by a mooning violation.

I think of hot-air ballooning as the most fear you'll ever experience in a wicker basket.

I told my relatives to think before they speak, and I haven't heard a word from them since.

Nudist camps are the perfect place for people who think regular camping just isn't horrible enough.

Periodically I like to re-enact a battle between the blue and the gray. But enough about my hair-tinting appointment.

Yeah, my pantyhose are baggy at the knees. My knees are baggy at the knees.

Styles come and go...unless you're a man.

I could've been a world-class sprinter if not for my knees. And my back. And my ankles. And my overall laziness.

Ah, the lazy days of summer. They rank right up there with the lazy days of spring, fall and winter.

Unfortunately, short-shorts are often also wide-wides.

I don't much mind when someone writes "wash me" on my car. It's when they shave it on the dog that steams my clams.

I took one of those memory courses. Now I can walk up to people I haven't seen in years and insult them by name!

The only thing wrong with public transportation is that it involves the public.

I gotta be me! I don't see anybody else lining up to do it.

Some people make you
wish that swimsuits
came with three pieces.
Or four. And
maybe a veil.

Why can't they invent
a pest repellent that
keeps the neighbor
kids out of my yard?

You can fool some of the people all of the time...so, find those people.

There must be a discount clothing store just for repairmen. Their pants are always 50 percent off.

The best way to
lose unwanted fat
is to get a divorce.

Lots of politicians
these days are true to
their convictions. But
that doesn't keep 'em
from wanting
early parole.

Throw a fit --
get a refund,
that's my motto.

A garage sale is what
you call junk that
hasn't made its way
out to the curb yet.

Chocolate is women's reward for putting up with men.

Ever notice how clothes that look great in a display window always lose that stylish "draped" look once you cram an actual body into them?

84

Hockey is my kind of sport! You need to be mean, and you don't need teeth.

Only one thing keeps me from staying on a diet. Food.

To me, getting on the information highway means I can cause traffic jams without leaving home.

Let a smile be your umbrella and you'll be wet as well as stupid.

You know you've wasted your money when the FBI warning was the best part of your rental video.

Here's a home remedy. Go home. Hey, it'll make me feel better.

I was going to get wall-to-wall carpeting installed, but I decided it would be cheaper to walk on 10-dollar bills.

For real enjoyment, nothing beats running... somebody else's life.

I work out every day.
Mostly frustrations
and anger.

I tried hypnosis to
quit smoking. Now
every time I light up
I quack like
a duck.

Having a meatball sandwich with the relatives seems somehow redundant.

Coffee is for people who feel they aren't irritable enough on their own.

I'm not cooking so much as I'm testing my smoke alarm.

I'll say one thing for big-screen TVs-- they're easier to hit with a coffee mug when you disagree with the talk show host.

I'm taking an anger management class, but the good-for-nothing jerk who teaches it really gets on my nerves.

Trying to "find yourself"? Look in the mirror, doofus. That would be you.

The weather channel is the perfect station for people who are too lazy to look out the window.

I went sledding the
other day, if you can
call the seat of my
pants a sled.

I like really dark
movie theaters. That
way I don't have to
buy my own popcorn.

It wouldn't kill me to be nice once in a while. But why take a chance?

If you were earning cash in your spare time, it wouldn't be spare time. It'd be work.

A day without griping is like a day without talking at all.

When somebody says, "Jump!" I say, "Down whose throat?"

There's a lot to be said for men. Of course it wouldn't be very ladylike to actually say it.

That "apple a day" thing isn't such a hot idea when your teeth are glued in.

I need to take vitamins in order to get the caps off my vitamins.

Apparently, they call it "alternative music" because it's the alternative to music that's good.

I take a lot of taxis. I love tellin' people where to go.

My idea of spring cleaning is to let the dog dust the furniture with his tail.

I don't talk to my pets like they're human... I don't even talk to humans like they're human.

It's tough walkin' the dog in this weather. His little nose keeps getting stuck to flagpoles.

Want to see a big fireworks display? Cut me off in traffic.

It's amazing how little paint it takes to make a neighbor's garden hose look exactly like a snake.

Here's a helpful tip for the winter--if you call out for pizza enough times, you don't have to shovel your walk.

Walk a mile in my shoes--then walk another mile--in fact, just keep the shoes and keep on walking.

You can't teach an old dog new tricks. And you can't sell them for much, either.

I've adopted a highway! Well, technically, I just drive like I own it.

I'd get my hair done, but my hair was finished years ago.

Golf isn't just a sport. It's a way of pretending you're getting exercise.

"You can't always get what you want." Unless what you want is "old" and "flabby." Most everyone can nail those two.

Thanks to "call waiting," we can now have unsolicited sales pitches interrupted by other unsolicited sales pitches.

Having a hot flash? Do what I do-- blame El Niño.

I'd make a really good phone psychic. I've been telling people what to do my whole life.

I should have been a lawyer. Shoot, I object to just about everything.

Nude skydiving is proof that you can be embarrassed and scared to death at the same time.

Is it me, or does the driver of the ice-cream truck always seem a little on the heavy side?

Do I have to claim the thousands of grocery store samples I inhale each year as income?

A true optimist is one who believes that fast-food employees always wash their hands after using the lavatory.

I figure if I was meant to cook, cars wouldn't fit through drive-throughs.

If you go long enough without brushing your teeth, any coffee can become flavored coffee.

I'll ask for a second opinion just as soon as I ask for a first one.

You can't judge a book by its cover, but you can read most of a magazine before the checker shows you out.

Fish make good pets because, in a pinch, they double as snacks.

For me "right wing" and "left wing" usually refers to the part of the bird the cat drags in.

Clipping coupons is a great way to save money. Especially if you appreciate deals like buying three gallons of mayonnaise to get the fourth gallon free.

If they can have a sneeze guard, why can't they have a grimy-kid-pawing-everything guard?

Just once I'd like to see a TV talk show that reunites the audience members with their brains.

Written by

Chris Brethwaite
Bill Bridgeman
Bill Gray
Allyson Jones
Kevin Kinzer
Mark Oatman
Dee Ann Stewart
and
Dan Taylor